This book
belongs to:

CREDIT
KIDZ

KIDZ BANK
1234 5678 9012 3456

BANK

KIDZ BANK
Debit Card
1234 5678 9012 3456
$5.00
+$1.00

tu
EQUIFAX
experian

NEW YORK STOCK EXCHANGE

LIABILITY
ASSET

TOYS
CANDY
CLOTHES
BUDGETING

ABC
DEF

Renting
Versus
Buying

www.ingramcontent.com/pod-product-compliance
Lightning Source LLC
Chambersburg PA
CBHW081710220526
45466CB00009B/2942
* 9 7 9 8 5 2 7 4 4 7 3 3 0 *